MINI CLASSICS

# THE OWL
### AND THE
# PUSSYCAT
And Other Nonsense Verse

© Parragon Book Service Ltd

This edition printed for:
Shooting Star Press, Inc.
230 Fifth Avenue–Suite 1212,
New York, NY 10001

Shooting Star Press books are available at special
discounts for bulk purchases for sales promotions,
premiums, fund-raising, or educational use. Special
editions or book excerpts can also be created to
specification. For details contact: Special Sales
Director, Shooting Star Press, Inc., 230 Fifth Avenue,
Suite 1212, New York, New York 10001.

ISBN 1 56924 199 6

Printed and bound in Great Britain.

MINI CLASSICS

# THE OWL
## AND THE
# PUSSYCAT
### And Other Nonsense Verse

## BY EDWARD LEAR
## ILLUSTRATED BY DOUGLAS CAMERON

SHOOTING STAR PRESS

# THE OWL AND THE PUSSY-CAT

The Owl and the Pussy-cat
went to sea
In a beautiful pea-green boat,
They took some honey,
and plenty of money,
Wrapped up
in a five-pound note.

The Owl looked up to
the stars above,
And sang to a small guitar,
"O lovely Pussy!
O Pussy, my love,
What a beautiful Pussy
you are, you are, you are!
What a beautiful Pussy
you are!"

Pussy said to the Owl,
"You elegant fowl!
How charmingly sweet
you sing!
O let us be married!
Too long we have tarried:
But what shall we do
for a ring?"

They sailed away,
for a year and a day,
To the land where the
Bong-tree grows,
And there in a wood a
Piggy-wig stood,
With a ring at the end of
his nose, his nose, his nose,
With a ring at the end
of his nose.

"Dear Pig, are you willing
to sell for one shilling
Your ring?"
Said the Piggy, "I will."
So they took it away,
and were married next day
By the Turkey who lives on
the hill.

They dined on mince,
and slices of quince,
Which they ate with a
runcible spoon;
And hand in hand,
on the edge of the sand,
They danced by the light of
the moon, the moon,
the moon,
They danced by the light of
the moon.

# THE POBBLE WHO HAS NO TOES

The Pobble who has no toes
Had once as many as we;
When they said, "Some day
you may lose them all;" —
He replied, —
"Fish fiddle de-dee!"

15

And his Aunt Jobiska made
him drink,
Lavender water tinged
with pink,
For she said, "The World
in general knows
There's nothing so good for
a Pobble's toes!"

The Pobble who has no toes,
Swam across the
Bristol Channel;
But before he set out he
wrapped his nose,
In a piece of scarlet flannel.

For his Aunt Jobiska
said, "No harm
Can come to his toes
if his nose is warm;
And it's perfectly known
that a Pobble's toes
Are safe, — provided he
minds his nose."

The Pobble swam fast and well,
And when boats or ships
came near him
He tinkledy-binkledy-
winkled a bell,
So that all the world
could hear him.

And all the Sailors and
Admirals cried,
When they saw him nearing
the further side, —
"He has gone to fish,
for his Aunt Jobiska's
Runcible Cat with crimson
whiskers!"

But before he touched the
shore,
The shore of the Bristol
Channel,
A sea-green Porpoise
carried away
His wrapper of
scarlet flannel.

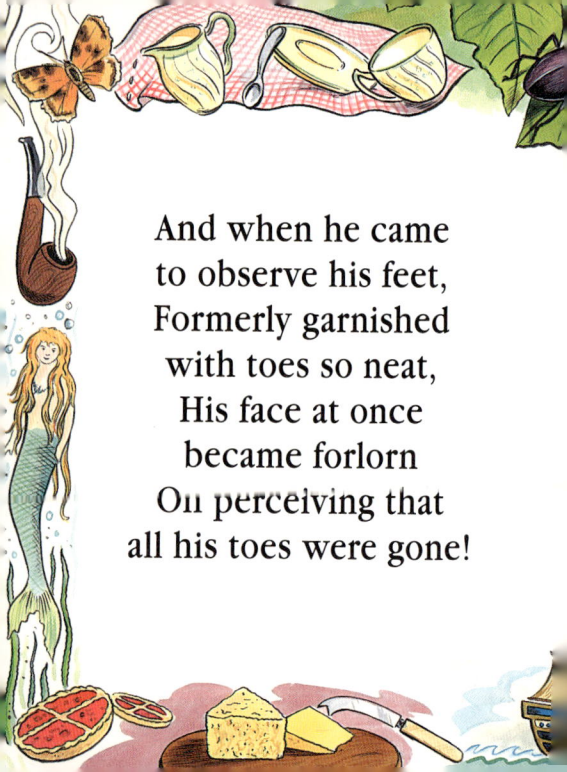

And when he came
to observe his feet,
Formerly garnished
with toes so neat,
His face at once
became forlorn
On perceiving that
all his toes were gone!

And nobody ever knew
From that dark day to
the present,
Who so had taken
the Pobble's toes,
In a manner so far
from pleasant.

Whether the shrimps or
crawfish gray,
Or crafty Mermaids stole
them away —
Nobody knew;
and nobody knows
How the Pobble was robbed
of his twice five toes!

The Pobble who has no toes
Was placed in a
friendly Bark,
And they rowed him back,
and carried him up,
To his Aunt Jobiska's Park.

And she made him a feast
at his earnest wish
Of eggs and buttercups
fried with fish; —
And she said, — "It's a fact
the whole world knows,
That Pobbles are happier
without their toes."

# THE QUANGLE WANGLE'S HAT

On the top of the
Crumpetty Tree
The Quangle Wangle sat,
But his face
you could not see,
On account of his
Beaver Hat.

For his Hat was
a hundred and two feet wide,
With ribbons and bibbons
on every side
And bells, and buttons,
and loops, and lace,
So that nobody ever
could see the face
Of the Quangle Wangle Quee.

The Quangle Wangle said
To himself on the
Crumpetty Tree, —
"Jam; and jelly; and bread;
Are the best food for me!
But the longer I live
on this Crumpetty Tree,
The plainer than ever
it seems to me

35

That very few people
come this way,
And that life on the whole
is far from gay!"
Said the Quangle
Wangle Quee.

But there came to the
Crumpetty Tree,
Mr and Mrs Canary;
And they said, —
"Did you ever see
Any spot so charmingly airy?"

"May we build a nest
on your lovely Hat?
Mr Quangle Wangle,
grant us that!
O please let us come
and build a nest
Of whatever material
suits you best,
Mr Quangle Wangle Quee!"

And besides, to the
Crumpetty Tree
Came the Stork, the Duck,
and the Owl;
The Snail, and the
Bumble-Bee,
The Frog, and the
Fimble Fowl;

(The Fimble Fowl, with a
Corkscrew leg;)
And all of them said, —
"We humbly beg,
We may build our homes
on your lovely Hat, —
Mr Quangle Wangle,
grant us that!
Mr Quangle Wangle Quee!"

And the Golden Grouse
came there,
And the Pobble who has
no toes, —
And the small Olympian
bear, —
And the Dong with
a luminous nose.

And the Blue Baboon,
who played the flute, —
And the Orient Calf
from the Land of Tute, —
And the Attery Squash,
and the Bisky Bat, —
All came and built
on the lovely Hat
Of the Quangle Wangle Quee.

45

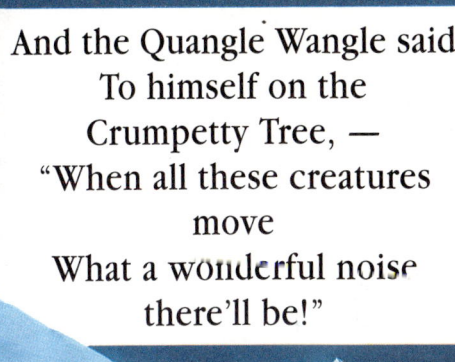

And the Quangle Wangle said
To himself on the
Crumpetty Tree, —
"When all these creatures
move
What a wonderful noise
there'll be!"

And at night by the light
of the Mulberry moon,
They danced to the Flute
of the Blue Baboon,
On the broad green leaves
of the Crumpetty Tree,
And all were as happy
as happy could be,
With the Quangle
Wangle Quee.

# THE JUMBLIES

They went to sea in a Sieve,
they did,
In a Sieve they went to sea;
In spite of all their friends
could say,
On a winter's morn,
on a stormy day,
In a Sieve they went to sea!

And when the Sieve
turned round and round,
And everyone cried,
You'll all be drowned!"
They called aloud,
"Our Sieve ain't big,
But we don't care a button!
We don't care a fig!
In a Sieve we'll go to sea!"

Far and few, far and few,
Are the lands where
the Jumblies live;

Their heads are green,
and their hands are blue,
And they went to sea in a Sieve.

They sailed away in a Sieve,
they did,
In a Sieve they sailed so fast,
With only a beautiful
pea-green veil
Tied with a riband
by way of a sail,
To a small tobacco-pipe mast;

And everyone said,
who saw them go,
"O won't they be soon
upset, you know!
For the sky is dark,
and the voyage is long,
And happen what may,
it's extremely wrong
In a Sieve to sail so fast!"

Far and few, far and few,
Are the lands where
the Jumblies live;
Their heads are green,
and their hands are blue,
And they went to sea
in a Sieve.

The water it soon came in,
it did,
The water it soon came in;
So to keep them dry,
they wrapped their feet

In a pinky paper
all folded neat,
And they fastened it down
with a pin.

And they passed the night
in a crockery-jar,
And each of them said,
"How wise we are!
Though the sky be dark,
and the voyage be long,
Yet we never can think
we were rash or wrong,
While round in our Sieve
we spin!"

Far and few, far and few,
Are the lands where
the Jumblies live;
Their heads are green,
and their hands are blue,
And they went to sea
in a Sieve.

All night long
they sailed away;
And when the sun
went down,
They whistled and warbled
a moony song,
To the echoing sound
of a coppery gong,
In the shade of the
mountains brown.

63

"O Timballo!
How happy we are,
When we live in a sieve
and a crockery-jar,
And all night long
in the moonlight pale,
We sail away
with a pea-green sail,
In the shade of the
mountains brown!"

Far and few, far and few,
Are the lands where
the Jumblies live;
Their heads are green,
and their hands are blue,
And they went to sea
in a Sieve.

They sailed to
the Western Sea, they did,
To a land all covered
with trees,
And they bought an Owl,
and a useful Cart,
And a pound of Rice,
and a Cranberry Tart,
And a hive of silvery Bees.

And they bought a Pig,
and some green Jack-daws,
And a lovely Monkey
with lollipop paws,
And forty bottles
of Ring-Bo-Ree,
And no end of Stilton Cheese.

Far and few, far and few,
Are the lands where
the Jumblies live;
Their heads are green,
and their hands are blue,
And they went to sea
in a Sieve.

And in twenty years
they all came back,
In twenty years or more,
And everyone said,
"How tall they've grown!
For they've been to the
Lakes, and the Torrible Zone,
And the hills of the
Chankly Bore";

And they drank their health,
and gave them a feast
Of dumplings made of
beautiful yeast;
And everyone said,
"If we only live,
We too will go to sea
in a Sieve, —
To the hills of the
Chankly Bore!"

Far and few, far and few,
Are the lands where
the Jumblies live;
Their heads are green,
and their hands are blue,
And they went to sea
in a Sieve.

## CALICO PIE

Calico Pie,
The little Birds fly
Down to the calico tree,
Their wings were blue,
And they sang "Tilly-loo!"
Till away they flew, —
And they never came back
to me!

Calico Jam,
The little Fish swam
Over the syllabub sea,
He took off his hat,
To the Sole and the Sprat,
And the Willeby-wat, —
But he never came back
to me!
He never came back!
He never came back!
He never came back to me!

Calico Ban,
The little Mice ran,
To be ready in time for tea,
Flippity flup,
They drank it all up,
And danced in the cup, —
But they never came
back to me!
They never came back!
They never came back!
They never came back to me!

Calico Drum,
The Grasshoppers come,
The Butterfly, Beetle, and Bee,
Over the ground,
Around and round,
With a hop and a bound, —
But they never came back!
They never came back!
They never came back!
They never came back to me!

# THE DUCK AND THE KANGAROO

Said the Duck
to the Kangaroo,
"Good gracious!
how you hop!
Over the fields
and the water too,
As if you never would stop!

"My life is a bore
in this nasty pond,
And I long to go out
in the world beyond!
I wish I could hop like you!"
Said the Duck
to the Kangaroo.

"Please give me a ride
on your back!"
Said the Duck
to the Kangaroo.
"I would sit quite still, and
say nothing but 'Quack,'
The whole of the long
day through!"

"And we'd go to the Dee,
and the Jelly Bo Lee,
Over the land, and over
the sea; —
Please take me a ride! O do!"
Said the Duck
to the Kangaroo.

Said the Kangaroo
to the Duck,
"This requires some
little reflection;
Perhaps on the whole
it might bring me luck,
And there seems
but one objection,"

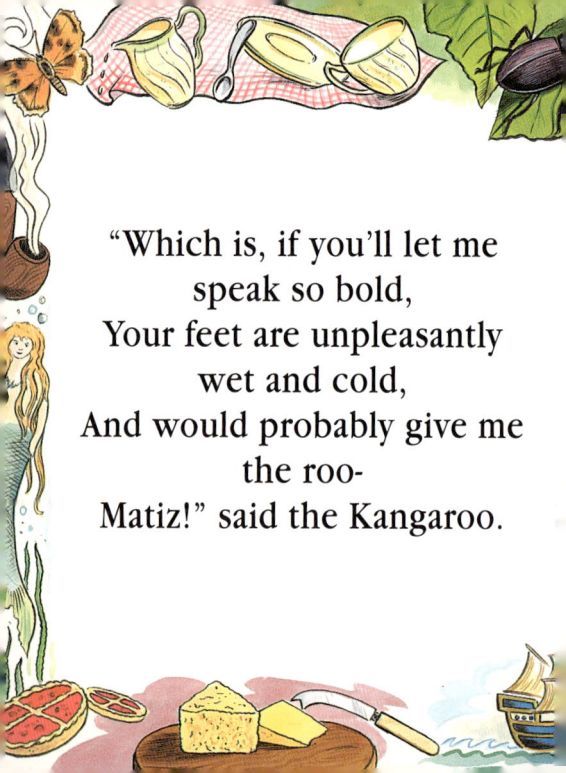

"Which is, if you'll let me
speak so bold,
Your feet are unpleasantly
wet and cold,
And would probably give me
the roo-
Matiz!" said the Kangaroo.

Said the Duck, "As I sat
on the rocks,
I have thought over that
completely,
And I bought four pairs
of worsted socks
Which fit my web-feet neatly."

"And to keep out the cold
I've bought a cloak,
And every day
a cigar I'll smoke,
All to follow my own dear true
Love of a Kangaroo!"

Said the Kangaroo, "I'm ready!
All in the moonlight pale;
But to balance me well,
dear Duck, sit steady!
And quite at the end
of my tail!"

So away they went
with a hop and a bound,
And they hopped the whole
world three times round;
And who so happy, — O who,
As the Duck and the
Kangaroo?

## Edward Lear

Edward Lear was born in London, England,
on May 12th, 1812. An artist by training,
he was better known for his nonsense verse
and limericks. The youngest of 21 brothers
and sisters, he enjoyed the company of
small children all his life. He wrote his first
nonsense rhymes for the grandchildren of
the Earl of Derby, whose collection of birds
he had been asked to paint. He scribbled
the poems at odd moments to amuse his
young friends and they were not published
until ten years later.
He was a shy and often sad man, whose
vivid imagination brought to life such
creatures as *The Jumblies* and
*The Pobble who has no Toes*.
He died in 1888.